SHIRLEY WILLIS was born in Glasgow. She has worked as an illustrator, designer, and editor, mainly on books for children.

BETTY ROOT was the Director of the Reading and Language Information Center at the University of Reading for over twenty years. She has worked on numerous children's books, both fiction and non-fiction.

PETER LAFFERTY is a former secondary school science teacher. Since 1985 he has been a full-time author of science and technology books for children and family audiences. He has edited and contributed to many scientific encyclopedias and dictionaries.

BOOK EDITOR: KAREN BARKER SMITH
EDITORIAL ASSISTANT: STEPHANIE COLE
TECHNICAL CONSULTANT: PETER LAFFERTY
LANGUAGE CONSULTANT: BETTY ROOT

AN SBC BOOK, CONCEIVED, EDITED AND DESIGNED BY
THE SALARIYA BOOK COMPANY, 25, MARLBOROUGH PLACE,
BRIGHTON, EAST SUSSEX BN1 1UB, UNITED KINGDOM.

ISBN 0-531-11826-6 (LIB. BDG.)
ISBN 0-531-15976-0 (PBK.)

FIRST AMERICAN EDITION 1999 BY FRANLKIN WATTS
GROLIER PUBLISHING CO., INC., 90 SHERMAN TURNPIKE, DANBURY, CT 06816

VISIT FRANKLIN WATTS ON THE INTERNET AT: HTTP://PUBLISHING.GROLIER.COM

A catalog record for this title is available from the Library of Congress.

GROLIER
PUBLISHING

CONTENTS

Wherever you see this sign, ask an adult to help you.

WHIZ KIDS
TELL ME HOW FAST IT GOES

Written and
illustrated by

SHIRLEY WILLIS

W

FRANKLIN WATTS
A Division of Grolier Publishing
NEW YORK • LONDON • HONG KONG • SYDNEY
DANBURY, CONNECTICUT

HOW CAN I RUN?

Your muscles make every part of your body move. Strong muscles help you run fast.

READY!

SET!

Go!

The harder your muscles
work, the faster you
can run.

We have muscles
all over our bodies.
You can feel your
muscles working.
Make a fist and
feel the muscles
at the top of your
arm bulge.

7

HOW DO WE MEASURE SPEED?

Speed is how fast things travel.
It is measured over an exact distance, like a mile or a kilometer.

READY, SET, GO!

Measure out a set distance and take turns to run. You'll need a stopwatch to time each run to find out who is fastest.

If you can run
1 mile in one hour,
your speed is
1 mile per hour.

I MILE AN HOUR
IS CALLED 1 MPH
FOR SHORT!

9

ARE FOUR LEGS BETTER THAN TWO LEGS?

Snails are the world's slowest animals. They travel at 0.03 mph.

Many animals can run faster than we can because they have stronger muscles. Animals have powerful muscles that help them run very fast.

10

Cheetahs are the world's fastest animals. They travel at 62 mph.

A CAT CAN RUN AT 30 MPH!

WHOOSH!

11

How Can I Go Faster?

Wheels make you go faster. A machine with wheels helps you make better use of your muscles.

The harder your muscles work, the faster the wheels spin around.

I CAN'T RUN AS FAST AS THIS!

PEDAL POWER

The harder you push on the bicycle pedals, the faster the wheels spin.

Bicycles and skateboards are machines with wheels.

13

WHY DOES OUR BALL SLOW DOWN?

As the ball rubs against the grass, it causes friction. This makes the ball slow down until it stops rolling.

Friction causes heat.
Rub your hands together
— do they feel warm?
Now try it with soapy hands
— they don't get so warm.
Slippery hands cause less friction.

Friction is caused
when things rub
together.
Friction makes things
slow down.

WHY DO SKIS SLIDE?

Snow and ice are very smooth. Skis are smooth, too. Skis slide easily because there is not much friction.

SMOOTH SURFACES CAUSE LESS FRICTION!

16

Without much friction,
it can be difficult to stop.

HOW CAN I SWIM FASTER?

When you swim, you cause friction in the water, which slows you down. You can swim faster if you cause less friction.

18

You cause less friction by moving through the water as smoothly as you can.

A long, smooth body shape glides through the water quickly.

Jumping into the water makes a big splash that slows you down.

TRY NOT TO SPLASH MUCH —IT SLOWS YOU DOWN!

WHY DO SOME BOATS HAVE SAILS?

Boats with sails use wind power.
When wind blows into the sails,
it pushes the boat along.

The stronger the wind,
the faster the boat can go.

20

SAIL AWAY!

You will need: A plastic tub
A plastic straw
Modeling clay
A piece of paper
Adhesive tape

1. Make a sail with the straw and paper (as shown).
2. Press a blob of modeling clay onto the bottom of the tub.
3. Push the straw into the clay.

WHY DO CARS GO FAST?

Cars go fast because
they have engines.
Engines are more powerful
than human or
animal muscles.

Air makes a moving car slow down.
Fast cars have smooth,
rounded shapes to help them
move faster through the air.

Fast cars have more
powerful engines
than slow cars.

23

WHAT MAKES TRAINS GO?

Trains are pulled by powerful engines. The engine power comes from electricity. The electricity comes from overhead electric wires or from a rail by the track.

A wire frame called a pantograph carries electricity from overhead wires to the engine.

ROAR!

WHY DO PLANES ROAR?

THAT NOISE HURTS MY EARS!

Planes have powerful jet engines that make them go very fast.

JET ENGINE

Burning gases rush from the back of a jet engine and push the plane forward at great speed.

Jet engines are powered
by burning gases.
As the gases burn,
they make a loud roar.

You can use air to make a loud noise. Blow up a paper bag and hit it very hard. It will explode with a bang.

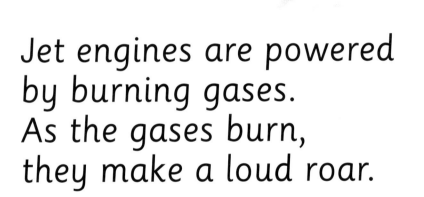

WHY DOES IT GO SO FAST?

Space rockets have the most powerful engines.
A rocket engine needs to be powerful enough to push a rocket into space.

Rocket engines are powered by burning gases. The burning gases push the rocket upward.

TO GO INTO SPACE, A ROCKET MUST TRAVEL AT 25,000 MPH!

28

LIFT OFF!

Blow up a balloon and let it go. As the air inside escapes, it pushes the balloon through the air.

29

GLOSSARY

distance   The amount of space between two objects or places.

electricity   A type of power that makes many machines work. It comes from electricity power stations.

engine   A device that drives many machines.

friction   A braking action caused when two things rub together.

jet engine   An aircraft engine that pushes hot gases out of the back of a plane to push the plane forward.

mile   A unit of length that measures 5,280 feet.

muscles   The parts of the body in humans and animals that make all movement possible.

pantograph   A device that feeds electricity to the engine of a train from the electric wires overhead.

rocket   A powerful machine that carries spacecraft into space.

sail   A piece of cloth attached to a boat that catches the wind and pushes the boat forward.

speed   How quickly something moves.

wind power   The power of the wind that makes an object move.

INDEX